Giggles, Gags & Groaners

Giggles, Gags & Groaners

By Joseph Rosenbloom
Illustrated by Sanford Hoffman

Sterling Publishing Co., Inc.
New York

To Sheila Barry

Rosenbloom, Joseph.
   Giggles, gags & groaners / by Joseph Rosenbloom ; illustrated by
   Sanford Hoffman.
      p. cm.
   Includes index.
   ISBN 1-4027-1755-5
   1. Wit and humor, Juvenile. I. Title: Giggles, gags, and groaners. II.
Hoffman, Sanford. III. Title.

PN6166.R77 2005
818'.5402—dc22

                                                         2004028509

Library of Congress Cataloging-in-Publication Data

10 9 8 7 6 5 4 3 2 1

Published by Sterling Publishing Co., Inc.
387 Park Avenue South, New York, NY 10016
Material in this book previously appeared in
Giggles, Gags & Groaners © 1987 by Joseph Rosenbloom
Distributed in Canada by Sterling Publishing
c/o Canadian Manda Group, 165 Dufferin Street
Toronto, Ontario, Canada M6K 3H6
Distributed in Great Britain and Europe by Chris Lloyd at Orca Book
Services, Stanley House, Fleets Lane, Poole BH15 3AJ, England
Distributed in Australia by Capricorn Link (Australia) Pty. Ltd.
P.O. Box 704, Windsor, NSW 2756, Australia

For information about custom editions, special sales, premium and
corporate purchases, please contact Sterling Special Sales
Department at 800-805-5489 or specialsales@sterlingpub.com.

ISBN: 1-4027-1755-5

Contents

1. Quick Quips 7
2. Sillies & Dillies 13
3. Law & Disorder 18
4. Yuck! 25
5. All Wet! 34
6. Totally Sick 42
7. Play It Again, Sam 50
8. Going Nowhere 58
9. Mother Nature Strikes Back 63
10. Monster Misfits 68
11. Play Ball! 73
12. You're Fired! 79
13. You've Got to Be Kidding 84
14. Fun Time! 89
 Index 96

1. Quick Quips

What is wrinkled, masked, and rides a horse?
The Lone Prune.

Did you hear the joke about the hole in the ground?
Never mind. You wouldn't dig it.

Did you hear the joke about the eraser?
Never mind. It would rub you the wrong way.

What is soft and cuddly and goes "Oink, oink"?
A teddy boar.

NIT: Somebody robbed the bakery yesterday.
WIT: Doesn't that take the cake!

MAN: Have you any dogs going cheap?
PET SHOP OWNER: No, sir, all our dogs go "Woof."

Why do elephants want to be alone?
Because two's a crowd.

What goes "Tick-tick, woof-woof"?
A watchdog.

What starts with an "*e*" and ends with an "*e*," but has only one letter in it?
An envelope.

Why was the letter "*e*" left back?
Because it was always in bed and never in school.

Did you hear about the romance in the post office?

A stamp was stuck on an envelope.

What did one gust of smoke say to another gust of smoke as it went up the chimney?

"I'm going out—can I borrow your soot?"

"Is your watchdog any good?"

"Oh, yes. If you hear a suspicious noise in the middle of the night, just wake him up, and he'll bark."

What did the hamburger say to the ketchup bottle?

"That's enough out of you."

How do cobras talk to each other?

Poison-to-poison.

What is yellow and goes "Ho-ho-ho"?

Santa Banana.

What is yellow and goes "Phut—phut—phut"?

An outboard lemon.

What is yellow, stands in a river during a storm, and doesn't get wet?

A canary with an umbrella.

Who went into the lion's den and came out alive?
   The lion.

What buzzed around King Arthur's head?
   The Gnats of the Round Table.

Did you hear the joke about the sandwich?
   Never mind. It's a lot of baloney.

What do Alexander the Great and Smokey the Bear
have in common?
   The same middle name.

What would you get if you crossed a duck with a
dog?
   A ducks-hund.

Where does a skunk sit in church?
In a pew.

Why did little Audrey wear only one boot?
Because she heard that the snow was one foot deep.

What time is it when four men are shoveling snow
with a policeman watching them?
Wintertime.

Why does it snow in the winter?
Because snow would melt in the summer.

How is a winter day different from an unconscious boxer?
One is cold out, the other is out cold.

What goes up when you count down?
A rocket.

What did the little zombie call his father?
Deady.

2. Sillies and Dillies

What is worse than being with a fool?
Fooling with a bee.

Which Muppet is hard to see through?
Kermit the Fog.

Little Audrey was taken to the museum by her
father. In one room filled with modern paintings,
there was a sign on the wall that read: "ART
OBJECTS." Turning to her father, little Audrey said,
"If Art objects, why is he letting them show his
paintings?"

What has sharp teeth, chops down cherry trees,
and founded a country?
Jaws Washington.

Visiting an observatory, the hillbilly watched the
astronomer look through his telescope. Just then a
star fell. "Wow-ee!" said the hillbilly. "Are you a
great shot!"

CUSTOMER: I want my money back.
CLERK: What's the problem?
CUSTOMER: I bought some birdseed here and it was no good.
CLERK: Wouldn't the birds eat it?
CUSTOMER: What birds? I planted every one of those seeds and not a single bird came up!

NIT: Have you ever seen an oil well?
WIT: No, but I've never seen one sick either.

Sign in front of clock repair shop:

CUCKOO CLOCKS
PSYCHOANALYZED CHEAP

SNAKE CHARMER: Be careful with that case! It contains a ten-foot snake.
PORTER: You can't fool me. Snakes don't have feet.

Did you hear about the two silly hunters? They came to a sign that said, "BEAR LEFT" and they went home.

FREDDY: I see your new microscope magnifies three times.
TEDDY: Oh, no! I've used it twice already!

"Doctor, I keep thinking I'm a horse."
"Well, I can cure you, but it's going to cost you a lot of money."
"Money's no problem. I just won the Kentucky Derby."

A man who had always wanted a parrot saw a pet shop with a sign that said: "GOING OUT OF BUSINESS AUCTION." Here, he thought, was his chance to get a parrot cheap. He went into the shop and, sure enough, there was a magnificent-looking parrot.

When the parrot was put on the auction block, however, the bidding went higher and higher.

Finally, the parrot was his!

The man left the store delighted with his purchase, but soon he had second thoughts. He had paid a lot of money for the bird. What if it wouldn't talk?

Back he went to the pet shop and demanded of the auctioneer, "Say, does this parrot talk? If it doesn't, I want my money back!"

Upon hearing this, the parrot spoke: "Not talk! Who do you think was bidding against you in the auction?"

Lem and Clem stood by a car in which they had locked the key.

"Why don't we get a coat hanger to open it?" Lem asked.

"No," answered Clem. "People will think we're trying to break in."

Lem said, "What if we use a pocketknife to cut around the rubber, then stick a finger in and pull up the lock?"

"No," said Clem. "People will think we're too dumb to use a coat hanger."

"Well," sighed Lem, "we'd better think of something fast. It's starting to rain and the sunroof is open."

3. Law and Disorder

What did the judge say when the skunk came into the courtroom?
"Odor in the court!"

JUDGE: You have a choice: Thirty days or a hundred dollars.
DEFENDANT: I'll take the money.

Who is the biggest gangster in the sea?
Al Ca-prawn.

What's purple, wrinkled, and carries a machine gun?
Al Ca-prune.

NIT: I'm never going to gamble again.
WIT: I don't believe you. You'll never quit gambling.
NIT: Want to bet?

A father wanted to cure his son of gambling. He asked the boy's principal for help.

The next day the principal called the boy's father. "I think I have cured your son of gambling," he said.

"How did you do it?" asked the father.

"Well, he looked at my beard and said, 'Sir, is that beard real or false? I wouldn't mind betting five dollars that it is false.' 'All right,' I replied. 'I'll take your bet. Now pull it and see.' Of course, my beard is real," said the principal. "He had to pay me five dollars. So I'm sure that will cure him of gambling."

"Oh, no!" groaned the father. "Last night he bet me ten dollars you'd let him pull your beard!"

Sign in a store window:

DON'T BE FOOLED BY IMITATORS GOING OUT OF BUSINESS! WE HAVE BEEN GOING OUT OF BUSINESS LONGER THAN ANYONE IN TOWN.

Another sign in a store window:

DON'T GO ANYWHERE ELSE
AND BE ROBBED—TRY US!

Why was the lamb punished?
Because it was baa-d.

What happened to the very bad egg?
It was eggs-secuted.

What did the egg say to the mixer?
"I know when I'm beaten."

MASKED MAN: Here's a thousand dollars.
POOR MAN: What's this for?
MASKED MAN: I steal from the rich and give to the poor.
POOR MAN: Wow! I'm rich!
MASKED MAN: All right—stick 'em up!

Why did the cucumber need a lawyer?
Because it was in a pickle.

Why did the strawberry need a lawyer?
Because it was in a jam.

PRISONER ONE: How long are you in for?
PRISONER TWO: Ninety-nine years. How long are you in for?
PRISONER ONE: Seventy-five.
PRISONER TWO: Okay, you take the cot by the door. You'll be getting out first.

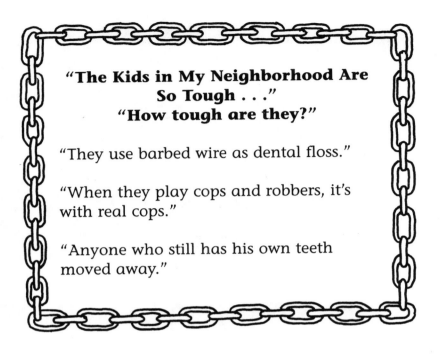

"The Kids in My Neighborhood Are So Tough . . ."
"How tough are they?"

"They use barbed wire as dental floss."

"When they play cops and robbers, it's with real cops."

"Anyone who still has his own teeth moved away."

What do you call a bird gangster?
Robin Hood.

What do you give someone who has everything?
A burglar alarm.

What is gray and goes around stamping out forest fires?
Smokey the Elephant.

To whom should you go for help when you're attacked by killer flies?
The SWAT team.

DIT: What were Tarzan's last words?
DOT: "Who greased the grapevine?"
DIT: Well, who did?
DOT: Oh, some grease monkey.

A policeman in a patrol car was astonished to see a woman knitting while driving her car. He drove up alongside her and called, "Pull over!"

"No," she called back. "Pair of socks!"

BOOKS FROM THE PRISON LIBRARY

The Gangster, by Robin Steele
My Life in Crime, by Upton O. Goode
Bad Money, by Count R. Fitz
You Always Get Caught,
    by Sue Nora Later

WATSON: What is your favorite tree, Holmes?
HOLMES: A lemon tree, my dear Watson.

What kind of ship do the police have to keep an eye on?
    A thug-boat.

4. Yuck!

A dog walked into a fast-food restaurant and ordered a thick shake. He drank it without fuss or delay and left.

The customers in the restaurant were amazed. One of them said to the clerk behind the counter, "That's quite a dog! Does he always do that?"

"Oh, no," the clerk answered calmly. "He usually orders a soda."

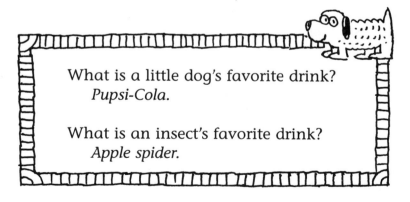

What is a little dog's favorite drink?
Pupsi-Cola.

What is an insect's favorite drink?
Apple spider.

Sign in front of an ice-cream parlor:

> **YOU CAN'T BEAT OUR MILK, BUT YOU**
> **CAN LICK OUR ICE-CREAM CONES!**

What bread wanted to rule the world?
Attila the Bun.

In a restaurant you must choose between eating an
elephant egg or a five-hundred-pound canary egg.
Which would you pick?
*A five-hundred-pound canary egg, because everyone
hates elephant yolks.*

What did the cow say when it had nothing to eat
but a thistle?
"Thistle have to do."

What is gray and powdery?
Instant elephant.

Can mustard be friendly with a hot dog bun?
Yes, if they have a frank relationship.

Where do extra-smart frankfurters end up?
On honor rolls.

Why couldn't the hamburger speak?
Because the catsup got its tongue.

What do cats like on their hot dogs?
Mouse-tard.

Who was the burger's all-time favorite movie director?
Sizzle B. DeMille.

 What do frogs eat with their hamburgers?
French flies.

How do you make a cream puff?
Chase it around the block.

Do you know what Mary had when she went out to dinner?
Everybody knows Mary had a little lamb.

What is convenient and weighs 20,000 pounds?
An elephant six-pack.

What is the difference between an Indian and an African elephant?
About 3,000 miles.

What is white and fluffy and swings from cake to cake?

A meringue-utan.

What do whales like to chew?

Blubber gum.

A newspaper columnist who wrote about money received a phone call from a stranger who spoke in an unusually low voice.

"I do not agree with you about the high cost of living," the voice said. "I'll have you know that my wife and I eat to our hearts' content for exactly forty-two cents a week."

"Forty-two cents a week!" exclaimed the columnist. "I find that hard to believe. How do you do it?"

A burst of static came over the telephone line.

"What's that?" said the columnist. "Please speak louder."

"I can't speak louder," said the voice. "I'm a goldfish."

How does a lion like his steak?
Medium roar.

A squirrel who lived in the zoo was leaning against a sign that read: "DO NOT FEED THE BEARS." A hand-lettered notice around the squirrel's neck read: "PLEASE FEED ME. I'M NOT A BEAR."

What kind of snack do little monkeys have with their milk?
Chocolate chimp cookies.

"Mother, may I leave the table?"
"Well, you certainly can't take it with you!"

What is a lemming's favorite dessert?
Lemming meringue pie.

What do you get when you cross a pig and a centipede?
Bacon and legs.

What do you get when you cross a dog and a chicken?
Barkin' and eggs.

What do you get when you cross a lighthouse and a chicken coop?
Beacon and eggs.

How do they tell that there's bread in the bakery?
They have a roll call.

Did you hear the joke about the week-old bread?
Never mind, it's too stale.

BOOKS FOR COOKS

Italian Food, by Liz Anya, Manny Kotty,
Minnie Stroni, and Lynn Guini
The Tin Can Cookbook, by Billie Gote
Stomach Cramps, by Henrietta Greenapple
Time to Eat!, by Dean R. Bell

What has bread on both sides and frightens easily?
A chicken sandwich.

What kind of sandwiches do cows like?
Bull-oney.

How do you keep peanut butter from sticking to the
roof of your mouth?
Turn the bread upside down.

What flies and wobbles?
A jelly-copter.

Why did the jelly wobble?
It saw the milk shake.

What made the biscuit box?
It saw the fruit punch.

What is long and skinny and short and round?
Spaghetti and meatballs.

What fruit rides in an ambulance?
A pear-amedic.

CUSTOMER: Waiter, there's a fly in my soup!
WAITER: No sir, that's the last customer. The chef's a witch doctor.

CUSTOMER: Waiter, there's a fly in my soup!
WAITER: Yes, sir. And if you push that pea over, he'll play water polo.

A frog went into a restaurant and ordered soup. When it was served, the frog turned to the waiter and complained, "Waiter, there's no fly in my soup!"

5. All Wet!

How do you keep from getting wet when you're in the shower?

Don't turn the water on.

What is gray and wet and lives in Florida?

A melted penguin.

Which animals goes "Cluck, bubble, cluck, bubble, cluck, bubble"?

A chicken of the sea.

What has four eyes and is very wet?

The Mississippi.

What lives under water and goes, "Dit-dot-dit-dot-dot-dit"?

A Morse cod.

What would you have if you crossed the Pacific Ocean with a chili pepper?
Heat waves.

What happens when you have an argument with a shark?
You get chewed out.

What old-time comedian do sharks like?
Groucho Sharks.

What kind of fish has two knees?
A tunee fish.

BOOKS FOR FISHERMAN

Waterways of the World, by Sue S. Canal
A Fish Story, by Czar Dean
Caught in the Flood, by Noah Zark
Little Fishes, by Anne Chovey

What fish goes shopping and drives a Porsche?
  A yuppie guppy.

What two fish are needed to make a shoe?
A sole and an eel.

What wears cowboy boots, holds two guns, and lives underwater?
Billy the Squid.

LITTLE AUDREY: How many fish have you caught, sir?
FISHERMAN: None yet. But I've only been fishing for an hour.
LITTLE AUDREY: You're doing better than the man who was here yesterday.
FISHERMAN: Really? How am I doing better?
LITTLE AUDREY: It took him five hours to do what you did in just one hour.

"For a quarter I'll imitate a fish," said the little boy.
"And how will you do that, my little man?" asked a lady. "Swim?"
"None of those cheap imitations," said the little boy. "I'll eat a worm."

Why do teakettles whistle?
Because they never learned to sing.

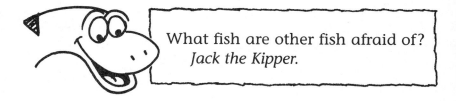

What fish are other fish afraid of?
Jack the Kipper.

SHAGGY DOG STORY

Two men were walking along the beach with a small shaggy dog. The dog's owner threw a stick into the sea. The dog immediately dashed after the stick by running on top of the water. He brought the stick back to his master.

The other man couldn't believe his eyes. "That is a very remarkable dog you have there," he said.

"Remarkable, my foot!" said the dog's owner.

"After all the lessons he's had, he still hasn't learned to swim!"

FISH WARDEN: That sign says: "NO FISHING ALLOWED."
LITTLE BOY: It's okay, I'm fishing silently.

What children live in the ocean?
Buoys and gulls.

How do the oceans cook?
By microwave.

What do mermaids like for breakfast?
Merma-lade on toast.

What is the difference between land and sea?
The land is dirt-y and the sea is tide-y.

What is the difference between a sailor and a
bargain hunter?
One sails the seas, the other sees the sales.

What do you get from an educated oyster?
Pearls of wisdom.

What sits on the bottom of the sea and makes you an offer you can't refuse?
The Cod-father.

TED: My cabin on the ship was nice, but that washing machine on the wall was terrible.
ALICE: Washing machine? That was the porthole!
TED: No wonder I never got my clothes back!

Did you hear the story about the water bucket with holes in it?
Never mind. I don't want it to leak out.

Did you hear the joke about the ocean?
Never mind. It's too deep for you.

Four-year-old Suzi, visiting her aunt's summer cottage, was watching a couple of water-skiers on the lake. Turning to her aunt, she said, "Those men are so silly. They're never going to catch up with that boat."

6. Totally Sick

Where do you take sick kangaroos?
To the hop-ital.

How do you take a sick pig to the hospital?
In the ham-bulance.

Where do you take sick puppies?
To the dog-tor.

PATIENT: Doctor, I feel like a dog!
DOCTOR: Sit!

DOCTOR: I have some good news and some bad news.
PATIENT: Tell me the bad news first.
DOCTOR: You have canary disease.
PATIENT: What's the good news?
DOCTOR: It's tweetable.

PATIENT: Doctor, I think I'm a bird.
DOCTOR: Well, don't get in a flap. Just perch on a chair.

PATIENT: During my operation, Nurse, I heard the surgeon use a four-letter word that upset me very much.
NURSE: What word was that?
PATIENT: "Oops!"

BABY SNAKE: Mommy, my head hurts!
MOMMY SNAKE: Come here and let me hiss it.

What do insects take when they are sick?
Ant-ibiotics.

"My dog's head is always hanging down, so I'm taking him to the doctor."
"Neck's weak?"
"No, tomorrow."

What quacks and runs his country with an iron fist?
A duck-tator.

What do elephants take when they get hysterical?
Trunk-quilizers.

What did the baby computer say when it got hurt?
"I want my da-ta!"

What is a computer's first sign of old age?
Loss of memory.

PATIENT: Doctor, can I sleep in my contact lenses?
DOCTOR: No, your feet would stick out.

What is gray, carries flowers, and cheers you up when you get sick?
A get well-ephant.

A traveling salesman, passing through a small town, saw a decrepit-looking old man sitting in a rocking chair on the porch of one of the houses. For all his years, however, the old man seemed so contented and happy that the salesman couldn't resist talking to him.

"You look as if you don't have a care in the world," the salesman said. "What is your secret for a long, happy life?"

"Well," replied the old man, "I smoke six packs of cigarettes a day, I drink a quart of whiskey every day, and I chew snuff. I never wash and I go out every night."

"That's fantastic!" exclaimed the salesman. "How old are you, anyway?"

"Twenty-five," was the reply.

BOOKS FROM THE DOCTOR'S WAITING ROOM

How to Make a Tourniquet, by Hank R. Schiff
Handling Your Emotions, by Mel N. Collie
Calm Down, by Ed G. Nerfs
Knocking Your Funny Bone,
   by Lord Howard Hertz

A little boy kept sniffling on his sleeve.

"Haven't you got a handkerchief?" asked an old lady.

"Yes, I do," said the little boy, "but I don't think my mother would like me to lend it to a stranger."

PATIENT: I don't think the pills you gave me are helping.

DOCTOR: Have you been taking them on an empty stomach?

PATIENT: Well, I've tried, but they keep rolling off.

What is the difference between a healthy rabbit and a sick joke?

One is a fit bunny, the other is a bit funny.

MOTHER: I'm so worried about my son. All he does is scratch himself and swing from a tree.

DOCTOR: Don't worry. He is perfectly normal—just going through a phase.

MOTHER: Oh, thank you, Doctor! How much do I owe you?

DOCTOR: Thirty bananas.

How does a train conductor sneeze?
A-choo! A-choo!

How does a tennis player sneeze?
A-tennis-shoe! A-tennis-shoe!

What is the difference between a person with a cold and a prizefighter?
One blows his nose, the other knows his blows.

What is red, white, and blue and good to have when you want to sneeze?
Hanky Doodle Dandy.

How is a sneezing elephant like a spy?
They both have a code in the head.

PATIENT: Doctor! I feel like a pack of cards.
DOCTOR: Wait here. I'll deal with you later.

"Doctor, you've got to help me! I was just playing the harmonica and I swallowed it!"
"Lucky you weren't playing the piano."

DOCTOR: What seems to be the trouble?
PATIENT: I keep thinking no one can hear me.
DOCTOR: What seems to be the trouble?

PATIENT: Doctor, I have a problem. I keep thinking I'm a bell.
DOCTOR: Take two aspirins and ring me in the morning.

"Doctor, Doctor, I keep thinking I'm invisible!"
"Who said that?"

7. Play It Again, Sam!

Which American march is heard in the jungle?
"Tarzan Stripes Forever."

How do elephants talk to each other?
By 'elephone.

What game do monster children play?
Hyde-and-shriek.

What has fuzzy pink ears and writes?
A ballpoint bunny.

What do yuppie rabbits want to be when they get
out of business school?
Million-hares.

Why was the clock thrown out of the library?
Because it tocked too much.

"I play checkers with my kangaroo."
"Does he ever win?"
"All the time. You should see him jump."

What is gray, has large wings and a long nose, and gives money to elephants?
The tusk fairy.

How is a song like a locked door?
You need the right key for both.

What game do hogs play?
Pig-Pong.

Little Harold was practicing the violin in the living room while his father was trying to read in the den. The family dog was lying in the den, and as the screeching sounds of Little Harold's violin reached his ears, he began to howl loudly.

The father listened to the dog and the violin as long as he could. Then he jumped up, slammed his paper to the floor, and yelled above the noise, "For pity's sake, can't you play something the dog doesn't know?"

What did the Beatles say when they saw the avalanche?

"Here come the Rolling Stones!"

What musical instrument is found in the bathroom?
  A tuba toothpaste.

What comes before a tuba?
  A one-ba.

What color is a guitar?
  Plink.

What elf was a famous rock star?
  Elf S. Presley.

An African chieftain flew to London for a visit. He was met at the airport by news reporters.

"Good morning, Chief," one of the newsmen said. "Did you have a smooth flight?"

The chieftain made a series of sounds—crackles, hisses, roars, whistles-and then added in perfect English, "Yes, pleasant enough indeed."

"And how long do you plan to remain in London?"
The chieftain began his reply with the same unusual noises and completed it in excellent English.

"Tell me," asked the reporter. "Where did you learn to speak such fine English?"

Again the chieftain repeated those strange sounds. "Shortwave radio," he said.

Sign outside a music store:

OUT TO LUNCH. USUALLY BACH BY ONE. OFFENBACH SOONER.

Sign outside another music store:

GONE CHOPIN, BACK IN A MINUET.

Sign outside a planetarium:

CAST OF THOUSANDS—EVERY ONE A STAR

What is beautiful, gray, and wears glass slippers?
Cinder-elephant.

What is the difference between Cinderella and a neat hairpiece?
One is a well-bred maid, the other is a well-made braid.

BOOKS FOR HOBBYISTS

Band Playing, by Clara Nett
Jazz Music, by Tenna Saxe
Cuddly Toys, by Ted. E. Behr
The Stars Tell It All, by Horace Cope
Sculpting the Gods of Greece and Rome,
   by Jove

MOE: I made a couple of pictures in Hollywood, but I had to stop.
JOE: Why? What happened?
MOE: My camera broke.

Lem and Clem were watching an old Lone Ranger film.

"I bet you ten dollars the Lone Ranger falls off his horse," said Lem.

"Don't be crazy," said Clem. "The Lone Ranger never falls off his horse."

"I bet he does."

"All right," said Clem, I'll bet ten dollars he doesn't."

They sat watching the film a few more minutes in silence. Outlaws began shooting. The Lone Ranger's horse reared, and off he fell.

"There! I told you!" shouted Lem.

"Oh, all right," said Clem. "Here's your ten dollars."

"No, I can't take it," said Lem. "I've got to be honest with you. I've seen this film before."

"So have I," Clem answered. "But I didn't think he'd be foolish enough to fall off twice!"

DIT: What was the worst part of the horror movie?
DOT: When I ran out of popcorn.

What is King Tut's favorite television show?
"Name That Tomb."

8. Going Nowhere

Why did the chicken cross the playground?
To get to the other slide.

What kind of elephants live in the North Pole?
Cold ones.

Why do elephants have trunks?
Because they'd look silly carrying suitcases.

What is yellow outside, gray inside, and very crowded?
A school bus full of elephants.

What do you get when you cross a watermelon and a school bus?
A watermelon that seats forty-five people.

What do you get if you cross a cactus and a bicycle?
A flat tire.

What do you get if you go stepping out with a five-hundred-pound canary?
   Stepped on.

What did one road say to the other road?
   "Hi, Way!"

What did the Wright Brothers say when they invented the airplane?
   "It's the only way to fly."

Sign in front of an auto body shop:

MAY WE HAVE THE NEXT DENTS?

PATIENT: Doctor, you've got to help me. I think I'm a bridge.
DOCTOR: Why, whatever has come over you?
PATIENT: So far, two trucks and a bus.

"Ma'am, your dog has been seen chasing a man on a bicycle."
"Nonsense, officer. My dog doesn't know how to ride a bicycle."

Why did the dog have to go to court?
He got a barking ticket.

Two big turtles and a small one went to have a root beer. It began to rain, and they decided that since the little turtle was the fastest, he should go home for the umbrella.

The little turtle objected. He was afraid that if he left, the big turtles would drink his root beer. At last they convinced him they'd leave his root beer alone, and the little turtle set out for home.

Three weeks passed. Finally, one of the big turtles said, "I'm getting thirsty. Let's drink that little guy's root beer."

"I've been thinking the same thing," said the other.

From the other end of the room, a little voice cried, "Oh, no you don't! If you do, I won't go home and get the umbrella!"

Did you ever wonder why people park their cars in driveways and drive them on parkways?

What is the egg capital of the world?
New Yolk City.

What egg goes to faraway places?
An eggs-plorer.

What do you say to a hitchhiking frog?
"Hop in!"

Sign outside a tailor shop:

**DON'T STAND OUTSIDE AND FAINT—
COME INSIDE AND HAVE A FIT!**

SIGN ON A DAIRY TRUCK:
From moo to you in
an hour or two

What do you call an elephant hitchhiker?
A two-and-a-half ton pickup.

Why are elephant rides cheaper than pony rides?
Because elephants work for peanuts.

Why don't elephants ride bicycles?
Because they have enough trouble riding their tricycles.

Where do people go dancing in California?
San Fran-disco.

Why did the chicken run?
It saw the fox-trot.

What does a frog say when it sees something great?
"Toadly awesome!"

9. Mother Nature Strikes Back

What has two tails, six feet, and three trunks?
An elephant with spare parts.

How do you transport cows?
In a moo-ving van.

Which three states have the most cattle?
Cow-lorado, Moo-souri, and Cow-lifornia.

What do you get when you cross a rooster and a duck?
A bird that wakes you at the quack of dawn.

Why did the rabbit go to the barber?
To get a hare-cut.

What eats cheese and buzzes?
A mouse-quito.

What kind of shoes do frogs wear?
Open-toad.

What do you call a funny chicken?
A comedi-hen.

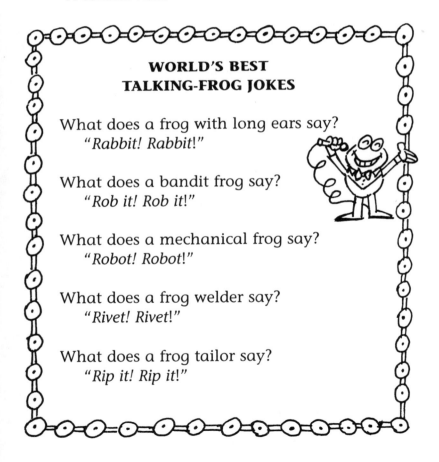

WORLD'S BEST
TALKING-FROG JOKES

What does a frog with long ears say?
"Rabbit! Rabbit!"

What does a bandit frog say?
"Rob it! Rob it!"

What does a mechanical frog say?
"Robot! Robot!"

What does a frog welder say?
"Rivet! Rivet!"

What does a frog tailor say?
"Rip it! Rip it!"

What did the chick say when it came out of the shell?

"What an eggs-perience!"

What order did the bird general give to his army?

"We-tweet!"

Why are elephants wrinkled all over?

Because they're too big to put on an ironing board.

What do you call a carrot who talks back to a farmer?

A fresh vegetable.

Which side of an apple is the reddest?

The outside.

What are spiderwebs good for?
  Spiders.

A diner in a restaurant called the waitress to his
table. Pointing to a sad-looking baked potato on
his plate, he said, "That potato is bad."
  The waitress picked up the potato and slapped it
roughly a couple of times. Then she put it back on
the diner's plate.
  "Now," she told the customer, "if that potato
gives you any more trouble, you just let me know."

What is big, purple, and has an English accent?
  Grape Britain.

GARDEN LOVE STORY

Do you carrot all for me?
You are my currant love.
My heart beets for you.
I'm melon-choly all the thyme when I don't
see you.
With your turnip nose, your radish hair,
and your cherry smile, you're a real peach.
My celery may be tiny, but weed make such
a swell pear.
If we cantaloupe, lettuce marry soon.
No sage would interfere.

10. Monster Misfits

How do Martians shave?
With laser blades.

What did the metric Martian say?
"Take me to your liter."

Why does E.T. have such big eyes?
Because he saw his phone bill.

What happened to the monster who ate the electric company?
He went into shock.

What do you get when a monster steps on a house?
Mushed-rooms.

What monster has the worst luck?
The Luck Less Monster.

When Godzilla goes out for dinner, what does he eat?

The restaurant.

Why did Godzilla eat Tokyo instead of Rome?
Because he wasn't in the mood for Italian food.

What did the monster say when it saw Santa Claus?

"Yum, yum!"

What monster is crazy about locks?
The Lock Nuts Monster.

NUTTY NONSENSE LIMERICK

A sea serpent saw a big tanker,
Put a hole in the side and it sank her.
It swallowed the crew
In a minute or two
And then picked its teeth
with the anchor.

YOUNG MONSTER: Mother, will I ever be able to join the army?
MOTHER MONSTER: No, but you can join the ghost guard.

What do little vampires need for all their toys?
Bat-teries.

What is a vampire's favorite circus performer?
An acro-bat.

Why do vampires drink blood?
Root beer makes them burp.

Where does Count Dracula get his jokes?
From his crypt-writer.

Did you hear about the new Dracula doll?
You put in a battery and it bites Barbie in the neck.

How do ghouls like their potatoes?
French fright.

What is a little ghoul's favorite game?
Corpse and robbers.

What is nine feet tall and flies a kite in a thunderstorm?
Benjamin Franklinstein.

When is a mummy not a mummy?
When it's a daddy.

What's green and spicy and changes into a monster?
Dr. Pickle and Mr. Hyde.

Why aren't vampires welcome in blood banks?
Because they only want to make withdrawals.

How many vampires does it take to change a lightbulb?
None, vampires prefer the dark.

What do you give a witch for her birthday?
A charm bracelet.

How did the two witches meet?
By chants.

11. Play Ball!

What did they call the dog that belonged to the baseball player?
The catcher's mutt.

Why did the batter take his car to the game?
It's a long drive to center field.

What do baseball players sing on third base?
"There's no place like home."

What is the difference between a rain gutter and a bad fielder?
One catches drops, the other drops catches.

How can you pitch a winning baseball game without throwing a ball?
Throw only strikes.

Little Arnold was pitching for the Little League team. After walking the first six players he faced, he was taken out of the game.

"It isn't fair!" he complained. "I had a no-hitter going!"

Arnold came home from playing ball, tears streaming down his face. When his father asked him what was wrong, he sobbed, "I was traded!"

"Don't feel bad about that, son," said his father. "Even the best baseball players get traded."

"I know," replied Arnold, "but I was traded for a torn glove."

ATHLETE: I have a weak back.
COACH: When did you first notice it?
ATHLETE: Oh, about a week back.

COACH: What this team needs is life.
MANAGER: Don't you think 30 days is enough?

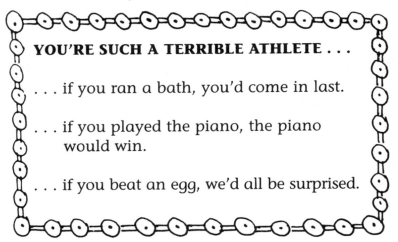

YOU'RE SUCH A TERRIBLE ATHLETE . . .

. . . if you ran a bath, you'd come in last.

. . . if you played the piano, the piano would win.

. . . if you beat an egg, we'd all be surprised.

A little boy knocked on the door of a friend's house. When the friend's mother answered, he said, "Can Georgie come out to play?"

"I'm afraid not," said Georgie's mother, "It's too wet, and Georgie has a cold."

"Well, then," said the little boy, "can his football come out and play?"

Did you hear about the long-distance runner who ran a 100-mile race? Well, he was in the lead and had only one more mile to go, but he was too tired to finish, so he turned around and ran back.

"I'm no longer the quarterback on our team."
"What happened?"
"It's all my mother's fault. She made me promise not to pass anything until somebody said 'Please!'"

COACH: Elmer, you can be the end, guard, and tackle.
ELMER: That's great, coach! Thanks!
COACH: Yes, sit at the end of the bench, guard the water bucket, and tackle anyone who gets near it.

COACH: Did you exercise this morning?
PLAYER: Oh, yes. I bent over and touched my shoes one hundred times.
COACH: You did?
PLAYER: Yes, then I took them off the chair and put them on.

REPORTER: What position do you play in the football game?
FOOTBALL PLAYER: Oh, sort of crouched down and bent over.

Did you hear the one about the miser who went to the football game because he thought a quarterback was a refund?

"What impressed you most about the opposing team?" the reporter asked the losing football coach.

The coach shook his head. "The fact that when they ran onto the field, it tilted in their direction."

The golfer had been having a terrible time. First he sliced the ball into some bushes, then into a trap, then across a highway. Finally he hit it deep into the woods. He went looking for the ball but couldn't find it.

"Why not forget it?" asked his caddy.

"No way," said the golfer. "That's my lucky ball!"

"Daddy," said the bright child accompanying his father on a round of golf, "why mustn't the ball go into the little hole?"

What has six feet and can't move?
Two yards.

Where should a jogger wash his sneakers?
In running water.

What happened when the jogger slammed into a pile of IOUs?
He ran into debt.

Did you hear the one about the boxer who was thirsty?
Someone beat him to the punch.

MANAGER (to fighter in ring): Don't be afraid of him. Just remember—if he were any good, he wouldn't be fighting you.

What smells nice and rides a horse?
The Cologne Ranger.

What tree knows kung fu?
Spruce Lee.

Who lives in a pod and knows kung fu?
Bruce Pea.

Why do soccer players get good grades in school?
They use their heads.

What did the bowling ball say to the bowling pin?
"I'll spare you this time."

12. You're Fired

"I hear you're not working for Mr. Smith any longer."
"I should say not—not after what he said to me."
"What was that?"
"You're fired!"

WANTED: TYPIST TO COPY SECRET DOCUMENTS MUST BE UNABLE TO READ.

Where do carpenters study?
Boarding school.

What is a carpenter's favorite dessert?
Pound cake.

What is St. Peter's favorite dessert?
Angel food cake.

Why didn't the farmer's daughter milk the mouse?
She couldn't fit the bucket underneath.

What happened to the kitten who fell in love with the Xerox machine?
It became a copycat.

Lem walked over to a ladder on which Clem was standing, painting the ceiling.

"Say, Clem," he said, "are you holding on tight to that brush?"

"I sure am," answered Clem.

"Well, in that case," said Lem, "I'd like to borrow the ladder for a few minutes."

What is a foot doctor's favorite song?
"There's No Business Like Toe Business."

What is a ski instructor's favorite song?
"There's No Business Like Snow Business."

What is the plumber's favorite song?
"Singin' in the Drain."

Why was the tiger made a sergeant in the army?
Because he had the stripes.

Which branch of the air force do birds join?
The parrot-troopers.

What is a miner's favorite game?
Mine-opoly.

What is an astronaut's favorite game?
Moon-opoly.

What did the computer say when it saw the programmers having a snack?
"Give me a byte!"

What do you get when you cross a computer programmer and an Olympic athlete?
A floppy discus thrower.

How do astronauts bring their food to work?
In launch boxes.

What happened to the plastic surgeon when he got too close to the fire?
He melted.

 What jackets do firemen prefer?
Blazers.

How is a firecracker like a jeweler?
They both make the ear ring.

What do they call cashiers in Shanghai?
Chinese checkers.

Who saw the lumberman cut down the tree?
The chain saw.

What is the difference between a butcher and a night owl?
One weighs a steak, the other stays awake.

What does a polite electrician say when you do him a favor?
"Thanks a watt!"

An elephant was walking down the street, looking depressed.

"Can I help you?" asked a policeman.

"I don't have a friend in the world," sobbed the elephant. "It's on account of my job. I work in the circus. I'm always dirty. I smell bad. And I work for peanuts."

"Have you ever thought of getting into some other line of work?" asked the policeman.

"What?" exclaimed the elephant. "And give up show business?"

13. You've Got To Be Kidding

What happened when the king's men played a joke on Humpty Dumpty?
He fell for it.

Why is a prune a better fighter than a hen?
Because a prune isn't chicken.

What do you call a chicken who's afraid of nothing?
Dinner.

What do they add to food in Saudi Arabia?
Sultan pepper.

Where do spies shop?
At the snoop-ermarket.

What do you get when big jungle animals go to the supermarket?

Long lions at the checkout.

Sign in a supermarket:

**PRICES ARE BORN HERE—
AND RAISED ELSEWHERE**

What do you get if you cross a stick of dynamite and an egg white?

A boom-meringue.

The policeman brought four boys before the judge. "They caused a lot of commotion at the zoo, Your Honor," he explained.

"I want each of you to tell me your name," said the judge, "and what you did wrong."

"My name is Harry," said the first boy, "and I threw peanuts into the elephant cage."

"My name is Larry," said the second boy, "and I threw peanuts into the elephant cage."

"My name is Gary," said the third boy, "and I threw peanuts into the elephant cage."

The fourth boy said, "My name is Peanuts."

What do you get if you cross an alligator and a parrot?

An animal that bites your head off if you don't give it a cracker.

"Pilot to control tower! Pilot to control tower! Pilot to control tower! I am circling the field. Please give me landing instructions!"

"Control tower to pilot. Control tower to pilot. Why are you shouting?"

"Pilot to control tower! Pilot to control tower! I don't have a radio!"

The passengers in the plane were startled to hear the pilot announce, "Ladies and gentlemen, do not be alarmed, but our Number One engine has developed a bit of trouble. We will be able to make the trip safely, but there will be a one-hour delay."

Ten minutes later, the pilot was heard again. "Ladies and gentlemen," he announced, "our Number Two engine has just quit. Do not be alarmed. We will make it, but there will be a two-hour delay."

Five minutes later, the pilot spoke again. "Ladies and gentlemen, our Number Three engine has died," he said. "Do not be alarmed. We can get to our destination, but there will be a three-hour delay."

Two minutes later the pilot came on the intercom again. "Folks," he said, "I'm afraid we have just lost our Number Four engine."

"On, no!" one of the passengers groaned to his neighbor. "I'm late for an appointment already! Now we're going to be here all day!"

JOHN PAUL JONES: I have not yet begun to fight!
FIRST MATE: No wonder we're losing!

Nine out of ten people who say the pen is mightier than the sword would rather be stuck with a pen.

PILOT: Mayday! Mayday! Two engines are on fire!
GROUND CONTROL: State your height and position.
PILOT: I'm five feet eight and I'm sitting in the cockpit.

14. Fun Time!

Two men met for the first time at a noisy party.

FIRST MAN: I'm sorry, I didn't hear your name.

SECOND MAN: Oh, my name is the hardest name you have ever heard.

FIRST MAN: I'll bet you twenty bucks my name is harder.

SECOND MAN: Okay. My name is Stone. James B. Stone. And that's hard!

FIRST MAN: I admit that name is hard, but my name is harder. And I win the bet.

SECOND MAN: Well, what is your name?

FIRST MAN: Harder, Samuel B. Harder.

What do you call six stones with electric guitars?
A rock group.

What is a musician's favorite ice-cream dish?
A root beer flute.

What do owls celebrate every October?
Owl-oween.

What do monkeys wave on Flag Day?
Star-spangled bananas.

What song did they play at the Easter Bunny's
wedding?
"Hare Comes the Bride."

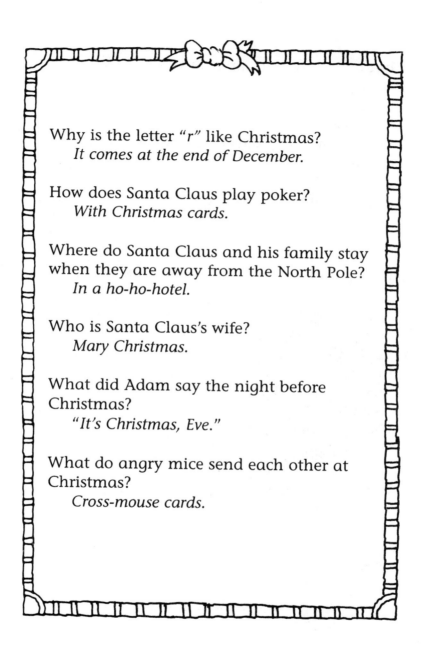

Why is the letter "r" like Christmas?
It comes at the end of December.

How does Santa Claus play poker?
With Christmas cards.

Where do Santa Claus and his family stay when they are away from the North Pole?
In a ho-ho-hotel.

Who is Santa Claus's wife?
Mary Christmas.

What did Adam say the night before Christmas?
"It's Christmas, Eve."

What do angry mice send each other at Christmas?
Cross-mouse cards.

What do you sing to a parrot when it's one year old?
"Happy Bird-Day to You."

What do cows like to listen to on the radio?
Moo-sic.

What kind of music do you hear in the playground?
Swing.

What kind of music do you hear at the paper-cup factory?
Dixie-land.

What kind of music do you hear at the Grand Canyon?
Rock.

Where do sheep go for sun and fun?
To the Baa-hamas.

How do baby chickens dance?
Chick-to-chick.

How do ghosts dance?
Shriek-to-shriek.

"Have you ever seen a barn dance?"
"No, but I've seen a chimney sweep."

While hiking, a Tenderfoot Scout and an Eagle
Scout came across an elephant.

"He should be taken to the zoo," said the Eagle
Scout. The Tenderfoot agreed.

The next day, the Eagle Scout saw the Tenderfoot
and the elephant were still together.

"You were supposed to take him to the zoo,"
said the Eagle Scout.

"I did," replied the Tenderfoot, "and today I'm
taking him to the movies."

Sign in front of a magic shop:

```
DISAPPEARED FOR LUNCH
```

What would you get if a prehistoric animal
swallowed a lemon?
    A dino-sour.

What prehistoric animal makes noise when it
sleeps?
    A dino-snore.

What would you get if a pair of dinosaurs crashed
into each other at sixty miles per hour?
    Tyrannosaurus wrecks.

What would you get if you crossed a dinosaur and
a witch?
    A Tyrannosaurus hex.

TEACHER: Danny, stop showing off and acting like a
fool! Who do you think you are—the teacher?

Wife to husband helping his small son with his
math homework: "Help him now while you can
—next year he goes into third grade."

Did you hear the joke about the shirt collar?
Never mind. I don't like dirty jokes.

Did you hear the joke about the dropped egg?
It cracks me up.

What did the stand-up comic say when he dropped an egg on his foot?
"The yolk's on me!"

WISE MAN SAYS:

A day without sunshine
is like night.

Index

Alexander the Great, 10
Astronomer, 13
Audrey, 11, 13, 37
Bakery, 7, 32
Baseball, 73–74
Bears, 10, 15, 30
Birds, 14, 16–17, 22, 42–43, 59, 81, 86, 92
Book names, 24, 32, 36, 46, 55
Boxers, 12, 77
Cars, 17, 23, 61
Cats, 27, 80
Chicken(s), 32, 34, 58, 84, 92
Cinderella, 55
Computers, 45, 81
Criminals, 18, 20, 21, 22, 24
Dinosaurs, 94
Doctors, 42–43, 45, 46–47, 48–49, 60, 81, 82
Dogs, 7, 8, 9, 10, 25, 31, 38, 42, 52, 60, 73
Eggs, 20, 26, 31, 61, 85, 95

Elephants, 8, 22, 26, 28, 44, 45, 48, 50, 51, 55, 58, 83, 93
Envelopes, 8, 9
Fish, 29, 35–37, 38, 40
Food, 9, 10, 25–33, 79, 89
Football, 75, 76
Gambling, 18–19
Games, 50–51, 81. *See also* Sports
Golf, 77
Holidays, 90–91
Horses, 7, 16, 78
Insects, 10, 22, 25, 33, 44
Judges, 18, 86
Kangaroo, 51
King Arthur, 10
Lambs, 20, 28
Lawyers, 21
Lions, 10, 30, 85
Monsters, 50, 68–72
Movies/TV, 56–57
Muppet, 13
Music, 51, 52–53, 81, 89, 92

Oil well, 14
Pigs, 7, 31, 51
Pilots, 87, 88
Policeman, 11, 23, 24, 83, 86
Rabbits, 46, 50
Santa Claus, 69, 91
Sick jokes, 42–49
Signs (store/shop), 14, 19, 26, 54, 59, 61, 85, 94
Skunks, 10, 18
Smoke, 9
Smokey the ..., 10, 22
Snakes, 9, 15, 43
Sneezing, 47, 48
Sports, 73–78
Tarzan, 23, 50
Tough kids, 22
Water jokes, 34–41
Whales, 29
Winter, 11–12
Work jokes, 79–83
Yellow, 9, 58
Zombie, 12